to be self-evident,

created equal,

by their Creator with

Rights, that among

Liberty and

of Happiness.

WENDELL MINOR

The Spirit of 1776 from A to Z

G. P. PUTNAM'S SONS

IN MEMORY OF MAJOR STEPHEN CHARLES REICH,
AND TO ALL AMERICANS WHO SERVE THEIR COUNTRY
TO PRESERVE OUR FREEDOM. —W.M.

America's Journey

Let's imagine that we live in colonial America during its fight to become a free nation, independent from England. When we travel, we have only horseback or stagecoach to take us on our journey. There are no cars, trains or superhighways. Only bumpy dirt roads connect the thirteen colonies. There are no large hotels or fancy restaurants along the way, just small roadside inns and taverns, known as public houses. We find hand-painted, wood-crafted signs hanging from posts outside the public houses that tell us we have arrived at a place to eat and rest after a hard day's journey. These signs are painted by local and traveling artists of the day, and often illustrate a person or place, an object or event that tells a story and welcomes travelers. When we step inside, we are greeted by the innkeeper and patrons who are anxious to share the news of the day. Since this is a time long before telephones, radio, television, and the internet, we must rely on the innkeeper, local townspeople, and other travelers to share the news of the colonies. We might learn of the "Sons of Liberty," Benjamin Franklin, Thomas Jefferson, or even King George III and England. We might hear news of General George Washington and the latest battle of the Revolution! If we're lucky, we might even hear a fellow patriot such as Patrick Henry give an inspirational talk to patrons sitting around the fireplace.

Let's follow the signs along a colonial road during the years 1765 to 1783 and learn about some of the people, places, and events that gave birth to our great nation.

Wendell Minor

A is for ACTS

The Stamp Act was one of several taxes imposed on the prosperous American colonies by Great Britain. The Stamp Act taxed all items made of paper: newspapers, pamphlets, playing cards, and legal documents. This tax so angered the colonies that it led to America's quest for independence.

An Emblem of the Effects of the STAMP

O! the fatal Stamp

B

is for

BOSTON MASSACRE

British troops were sent to Boston to control the colonists. Violence erupted when British soldiers fired into a crowd of patriot protesters, killing five of them. The first to die was Crispus Attucks, an African American sailor and runaway slave, who became the first hero of the American Revolution. This event further fanned the flames of America's desire to be free of British control.

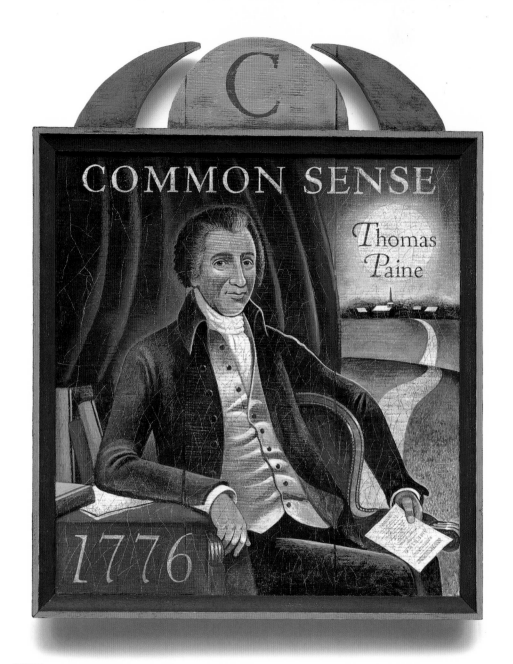

C is for COMMON SENSE

Patriot Thomas Paine wrote a pamphlet called *Common Sense*, which was widely read by the colonists. Paine wrote with great passion about his belief that America should seek its own destiny without British rule.

He wrote, "The sun never shined on a cause of greater worth."

D is for DECLARATION

The Declaration of Independence expressed the beliefs of a new nation in unforgettable language. Thomas Jefferson completed the first draft in one day.

When delegates of the Second Continental Congress gathered in Philadelphia on July 4, John Hancock was the first to sign the document, and his signature is the most notable.

E

is for

EAST INDIA COMPANY

A group of young patriots called the Sons of Liberty, disguised as Mohawks, boarded three ships owned by the English East India Company in Boston Harbor. The "Mohawks" threw 342 chests of tea overboard, protesting unfair taxes on the imports. At the "Boston Tea Party" colonists celebrated by singing, "Rally, Mohawks! Bring out your axes, and tell King George we'll pay no taxes!"

THE
BOSTON
TEA PARTY
1773

EAST
INDIA
TEA

F
is for
FRANKLIN

Benjamin Franklin had no formal education beyond the age of ten. He began to work at age eight as a printer and loved to read and write. He ran away to Philadelphia, where he became an inventor, scientist, printer, publisher, diplomat, and founder of the first lending library in America. He helped draft the Declaration of Independence.

Franklin wrote, "If you would not be forgotten, as soon as you are dead and rotten, either write things worth reading or do things worth writing."

FRANKLIN

G is for George III

George III was the King of England during the Revolutionary War. He was determined to keep the American colonies under English rule, and was nicknamed "the Royal Brute" by Thomas Paine.

The sign of the Green Dragon hung outside a tavern in Boston where Paul Revere and the Sons of Liberty met in secret to plot against King George.

THE
GREEN
DRAGON

KING
GEORGE
III

H is for HENRY

Patrick Henry, one of the Sons of Liberty, was a fiery, spellbinding speaker. As a delegate to the Virginia Convention, he shouted, "Give me liberty or give me death!" in one of the most famous speeches ever given in American history. As a result of that speech, a resolution was passed to send the Virginia militia to the aid of Massachusetts.

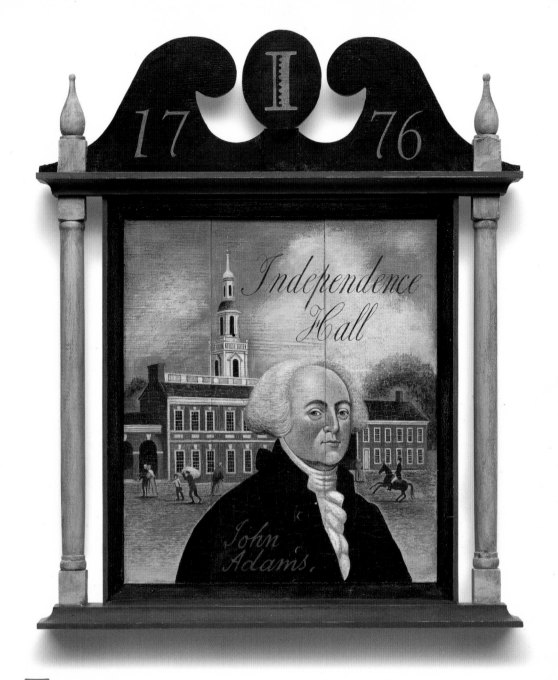

I is for INDEPENDENCE

Originally called Pennsylvania's State House, Independence Hall was colonial America's grandest public building and the meeting place where the Second Continental Congress declared independence from England. John Adams was one of five delegates appointed to write the declaration. In one of his last public statements, Adams declared, "Independence forever!"

J

is for

JEFFERSON

Thomas Jefferson drafted the Declaration of Independence at the Indian Queen Tavern in Philadelphia. He was an architect, naturalist, gardener, scientist, farmer, and horseman. He loved books and was the founder of the first state university in Virginia. In a letter to his friend John Adams, he once wrote, "I cannot live without books." In an amazing coincidence, he and John Adams died on the same day—July 4, 1826.

Thomas Jefferson was America's third president.

K is for Knox

Henry Knox was a bookseller who specialized in military books and later became colonel of the Continental Artillery. Colonel Knox and his men used oxen-driven sleds to haul fifty-nine cannons, which had been captured at Fort Ticonderoga, more than 300 miles to fight the British army in Boston.

Colonel Knox and General Washington became close friends and served together throughout the war. Knox was one of the first Americans to call George Washington the "Father of His Country."

Knox's Cannons

1776

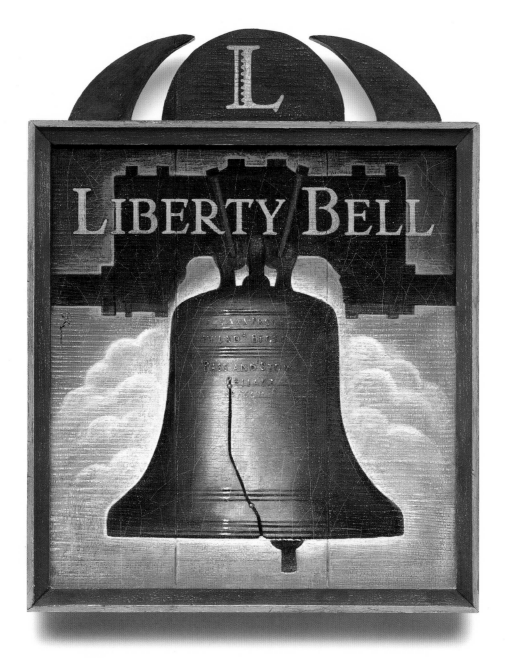

L is for LIBERTY

America's most famous symbol of freedom, the Liberty Bell in Pennsylvania's State House rang out to announce the first public reading of the Declaration of Independence. It cracked many years later while ringing to celebrate George Washington's birthday. The inscription cast on the bell reads, "Proclaim Liberty throughout all the land unto all the inhabitants thereof."

M is for MILITIA

The militia was made up of farmers and townsmen. These volunteer soldiers were the first line of defense against the British troops before there was a Continental Army. The Revolution began in Massachusetts when eight militiamen lost their lives fighting the British on the Lexington Green. The Massachusetts militia carried their New England pine tree flag to the battle of Bunker Hill.

N is for NATIVE AMERICAN

The Revolution split Native Americans into different sides. Although many Native Americans fought with the colonists, most sided with the British in the hope of protecting their homeland from being taken over by the colonists.

Native American Joseph Brant was a Mohawk chief who said:

"Every man of us thought that, by fighting for the King, we should ensure for ourselves and our children a good inheritance."

O

is for

Old North Church

On the night of April 18, 1775, Paul Revere instructed the rector of Old North Church in Boston to light one lantern in the steeple window to warn the patriots if the British army was coming by land and to light two lanterns if they were coming "by sea." British troops crossed Back Bay in longboats and traveled north to Lexington and Concord to seize the colonists' weapons. The next morning, the Massachusetts militiamen were ready to face the British and the Revolution began with the "shot heard round the world."

P

is for

PITCHER

"Molly Pitcher" was a nickname given to Mary Ludwig Hays, one of many women who made valuable contributions to the Revolution. During the battle of Monmouth, the fighting and heat were intense, and Mary carried water to the wounded soldiers. When her husband was wounded, Mary took his position with his gun crew so that they could keep their cannon firing at the British. Thereafter, she was hailed as "Sergeant Molly."

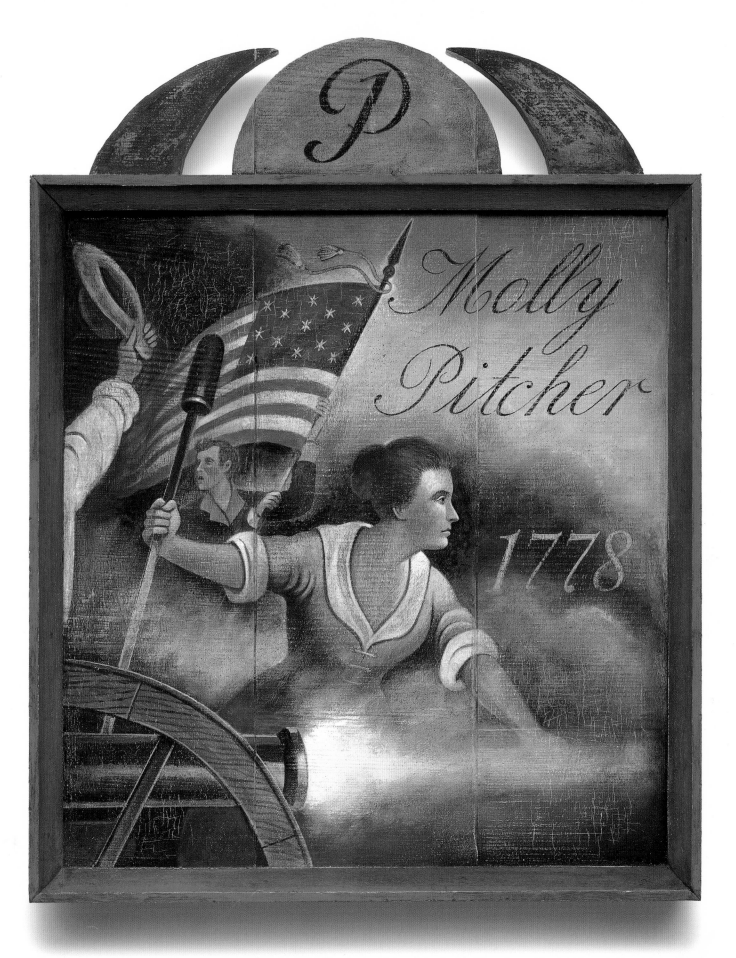

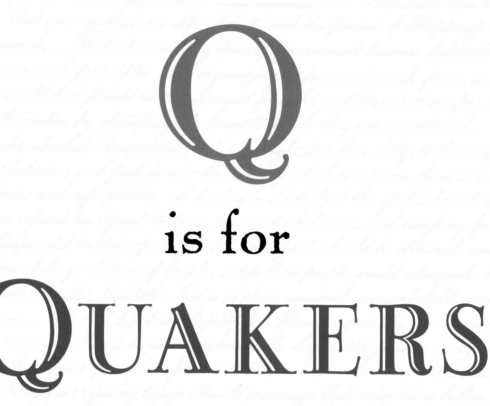

Q is for QUAKERS

Quakers were prosperous farmers who believed in religious freedom, and who thought that war was wrong. However, a few Quakers put aside their beliefs for the defense of the new nation, including one of the Continental Army's greatest generals, Nathanael Greene.

The Quakers were among the first groups of colonists to promote freedom for slaves in colonial America.

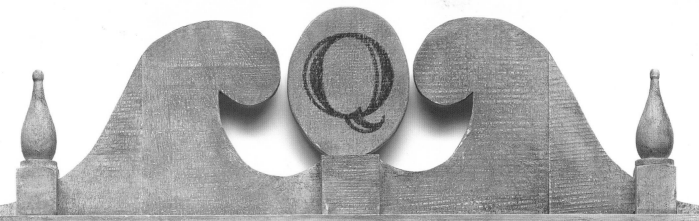

R is for REVERE

Paul Revere was an artist and a silversmith who led the Sons of Liberty. As a secret agent for the patriots, Revere received word that British troops were en route to take their weapons. That night he rode his horse from Boston to Lexington, Massachusetts, where he warned John Hancock and Samuel Adams to prepare the citizens for battle.

S is for STARS AND STRIPES

On June 14, 1777, Congress passed the Flag Act to establish an official flag for the new nation. The first flag had thirteen red and white stripes and thirteen white stars on a blue field, representing the colonies. It has been suggested that red represents courage, white represents purity, and blue represents justice. Every June 14, America celebrates Flag Day.

T is for TRENTON

On Christmas night of 1776, General Washington's army crossed the Delaware River in longboats in the sleet and snow to conduct a secret raid on the German soldiers fighting for the British in Trenton, New Jersey. The next morning, so taken by surprise was the enemy that the fighting was over in less than an hour. This was an important victory for Washington and his men, who had suffered many defeats that year, and it gave the Continental Army renewed hope to carry on.

T

Battle of Trenton
1776

U
is for
UNITED

The name the United States of America was first used in the Declaration of Independence. In 1782, Secretary of Congress Charles Thomson designed the Great Seal of the United States with an eagle carrying a banner in its beak with the Latin phrase "E pluribus unum," which means "Out of many, one."

UNITED STATES

1782

V

is for
Valley Forge

General Washington's troops traveled twenty miles from Philadelphia to Valley Forge to set up winter camp in December 1777. His soldiers experienced severe shortages of food, clothing, fresh water, and medical supplies and more than two thousand died. Nonetheless, Washington's troops pulled together and gained new strength and new volunteers after that terrible winter to become a more unified fighting force.

W is for WASHINGTON

After winning the War of Independence, General Washington gave an emotional farewell speech to his officers at the Fraunces Tavern in New York City. He returned to Virginia, where he placed a dove of peace weather vane atop Mount Vernon, the beloved home he shared with his wife, Martha.

George Washington became America's first president in 1789.

X is for X REGIMENT

The Roman numeral X represents the British Tenth Regiment of Foot, who sought to control the colonists in Boston. This regiment took part in battles at Lexington, Concord, Bunker Hill, and Monmouth. Officers of the Tenth Regiment wore on their uniforms crossed belts with buckles displaying a large X.

Y is for YORKTOWN

America won the last major battle of the Revolution at Yorktown, Virginia, when British General Cornwallis's army surrendered to General Washington's army. Hope for a British victory in the war against America was lost.

Z
is for
ZANE

In the fall of 1782, British troops and their Indian allies conducted one final attack on Fort Henry in Ohio. Patriot Colonel Ebenezer Zane and his men were running low on gunpowder. It is legend that Zane's sixteen-year-old sister, Elizabeth, risked her life to fetch more powder and saved the day.

Z

1782

ELIZABETH ZANE

AMERICAN REVOLUTION
SOME IMPORTANT DATES

The original thirteen colonies—Connecticut, Delaware, Georgia, Maryland, Massachusetts, New Hampshire, New Jersey, New York, North Carolina, Pennsylvania, Rhode Island, South Carolina and Virginia—gave birth to a new nation we know as the United States of America. Today, there are 50 states, but the rich history of the American Revolution belongs to the states that represent the circle of 13 stars on America's first official flag of 1777.

1765
★ The Stamp Act is passed by English Parliament in March and angers the colonists, who do not want to pay taxes directly to England.
★ The Sons of Liberty, an underground organization opposed to the Stamp Act, is formed in a number of colonial towns.

1768
★ British troops arrive in Boston, Massachusetts, in July to keep order.

1770
★ The Boston Massacre occurs March 5 when a mob of colonists insult the British troops, who then fire into the crowd, killing five protesters.

1773
★ The Boston Tea Party takes place December 16 when Paul Revere and the Sons of Liberty board British ships in Boston Harbor and throw cases of tea overboard to protest import taxes.

1774
★ The First Continental Congress meets in Philadelphia, with delegates representing every one of the thirteen colonies except Georgia. George Washington, Samuel Adams, Patrick Henry and John Hancock all attend.

1775
★ The American Revolution officially begins on April 19 when the "shot heard round the world" is fired on the Lexington Green in Massachusetts at the battles of Lexington and Concord. The night before, Paul Revere, Samuel Prescott and William Dawes had been sent from Boston to warn the citizens of Lexington that the British were coming.
★ American forces capture Fort Ticonderoga in New York on May 10, which contains a large supply of weapons.
★ The Second Continental Congress appoints George Washington general and commander in chief of the new Continental Army on June 15.
★ The battle of Bunker Hill is fought in Boston on June 17 and is the first major fight of the war.

1776
- ★ Thomas Paine's best seller *Common Sense* is published in Philadelphia in January, urging colonists to support American independence.
- ★ Henry Knox transports cannons captured at Fort Ticonderoga from New York to Boston, and by March the British evacuate Boston.
- ★ On July 4, the Declaration of Independence is adopted by Congress and signed by John Hancock; most members of Congress sign it August 2.
- ★ The first public reading of the Declaration occurs on July 8 in Philadelphia.
- ★ General Washington and his army cross the Delaware River on Christmas night and capture Trenton, New Jersey.

1777
- ★ On June 14, Congress issues a resolution to create our first national flag.
- ★ General Washington's troops set up winter camp at Valley Forge.

1778
- ★ The American Revolution officially becomes a world war when France comes to the aid of America in February.
- ★ "Molly Pitcher" fights in the battle of Monmouth in New Jersey on June 27 and 28.

1780
- ★ The British capture Charleston, South Carolina, on May 12 in the worst American defeat of the Revolutionary War.
- ★ General Washington names Nathanael Greene commander of the Southern Army on October 14.

1781
- ★ The British troops surrender to American forces at Yorktown, Virginia, on October 19.

1782
- ★ Congress adopts the Great Seal of the United States on June 20.
- ★ The final battle of the Revolutionary War occurs on November 10 in Ohio territory.

1783
- ★ Congress declares the official end of the Revolutionary War on April 11.
- ★ General George Washington delivers his farewell speech to his troops, and the Continental Army disbands.

AFTERWORD ★ I hope that you have enjoyed your journey of discovery on America's colonial roads. There is, of course, much more to learn, and the titles below will give you some helpful sources with which to explore further the history of the American Revolution. I wish you a very pleasant journey on your own road of discovery. —W. M.

SOURCES

Fleming, Thomas. *Liberty! The American Revolution.* Viking, 1997.

Grafton, John. *The American Revolution.* Dover Publications, Inc., 1975.

Hamburger, Kenneth E., Joseph R. Fischer, and Steven C. Gravlin.
    Why America Is Free. The Society of the Cincinnati, 1998.

Herbert, Janis. *The American Revolution for Kids.* Chicago Review Press, 2002.

McCullough, David. *John Adams.* Simon & Schuster, 2001.

McCullough, David. *1776.* Simon & Schuster, 2005.

Mastai, Boleslaw, and Marie-Louise D'Otrange Mastai. *The Stars and the Stripes.* Alfred A. Knopf, 1973.

Murray, Stuart. *America's Song: The Story of "Yankee Doodle."* Images from the Past, 1999.

Murray, Stuart. *American Revolution.* DK Publishing, Inc., 2002.

Schoelwer, Susan P., ed. *Lions & Eagles & Bulls: Early American Tavern & Inn Signs.*
    The Connecticut Historical Society/Princeton University Press, 2000.

Sedeen, Margaret. *Star-Spangled Banner: Our Nation and Its Flag.* National Geographic Society, 1993.

Thompson, John M. *The Revolutionary War.* National Geographic Society, 2004.

ACKNOWLEDGMENTS ★ A very special thanks to my longtime friend David McCullough, who has brought to millions of readers a great gift in his brilliant recounting of America's birth. Reading and designing the covers for *John Adams* and *1776* was not only a pleasure, but a true source of inspiration. ★ I wish to thank master woodworker John Reichling for constructing the beautiful wooden sign replicas so that I might assume the role of early American artist and sign painter. The two distinct sign shapes found in this book are typical of the ones commonly found in America in the eighteenth century. ★ I am grateful to William Martin, author of *Citizen Washington,* for his advice in offering many topic suggestions from A to Z. Also thanks to Dick Ayer for bringing a history teacher's perspective to my attention while considering all the possibilities for *Yankee Doodle America.* ★ Thanks to Gamma One for shooting and retouching the transparencies of the three-dimensional art of this book. ★ Thanks to my editor, Nancy Paulsen, publisher, Doug Whiteman, art director, Cecilia Yung, and designer, Gunta Alexander, for their continued support and expertise. They always make the process of creating a book a very gratifying experience.

G. P. PUTNAM'S SONS A division of Penguin Young Readers Group.

Published by The Penguin Group. Penguin Group (USA) Inc., 375 Hudson Street, New York, NY 10014, U.S.A.

Penguin Group (Canada), 90 Eglinton Avenue East, Suite 700, Toronto, Ontario, Canada M4P 2Y3 (a division of Pearson Penguin Canada Inc.). Penguin Books Ltd, 80 Strand, London WC2R 0RL, England. Penguin Ireland, 25 St. Stephen's Green, Dublin 2, Ireland (a division of Penguin Books Ltd.). Penguin Group (Australia), 250 Camberwell Road, Camberwell, Victoria 3124, Australia (a division of Pearson Australia Group Pty Ltd). Penguin Books India Pvt Ltd, 11 Community Centre, Panchsheel Park, New Delhi - 110 017, India. Penguin Group (NZ), Cnr Airborne and Rosedale Roads, Albany, Auckland 1310, New Zealand (a division of Pearson New Zealand Ltd). Penguin Books (South Africa) (Pty) Ltd, 24 Sturdee Avenue, Rosebank, Johannesburg 2196, South Africa. Penguin Books Ltd, Registered Offices : 80 Strand, London WC2R 0RL, England.

Library of Congress Cataloging-in-Publication Data   Minor, Wendell. Yankee Doodle America : the spirit of 1776 from A to Z / Wendell Minor.   p. cm. Includes bibliographical references. 1. United States—History—Revolution, 1775–1783—Juvenile literature. 2. Alphabet books—Juvenile literature. I. Title. E208.M534 2006   973.3—dc22   2005025174   ISBN 0-399-24003-9   10 9 8 7 6 5 4 3 2 1   First Impression

We hold these truths
that all men are
that they are endowed
certain unalienable
these are Life,
the pursuit